Roman Skowranek

Lighting Design

Roman Skowranek

Lighting Design

BIRKHÄUSER
BASEL

Contents

Foreword

Light is an essential design element in architectural planning. Natural and artificial light illuminate architecture as a whole or in detail, creating atmospheric moods and enabling the optimal use of a space. The demands for lighting planning are as diverse as the expectations and needs of users. For example, those working on computers require a glare-free and generally bright environment, while watchmakers or goldsmiths need targeted lighting. In commercial settings, lighting moods and colors are adjusted according to the product presented, whereas in cinemas or cozy cafés, soft and pleasantly warm light is required. The illumination of exterior and interior spaces is therefore an important topic in architecture that extends far beyond purely technical implementation and calculation. Intelligent design solutions help to develop design requirements, functions, and technology into a holistic solution in order to reduce the energy requirement of the building, for instance by the use of natural lighting.

Thus, lighting planning has developed into a distinct professional field in recent years. In order to be able to consider the guiding principles in the design right from the outset, a broad knowledge of the requirements and possibilities of lighting planning is necessary. In addition to the technical systems, this includes, above all, an understanding of the relationships and the use of the right specifications for specific tasks. It is vital to understand the concept of illumination and lighting as an integral part of any design. *Basics Lighting Design* provides a compact and wide-ranging introduction, allowing the reader to integrate this knowledge into their designs.

Bert Bielefeld, Editor

Introduction

Light is of vital importance for human beings. For in addition to our ability to see, our bio- and circadian rhythms are shaped by light. The Importance of Lighting Design

Hence, within the context of planning buildings and exterior spaces, light planning is not only a central element in design, it is also of immense importance to the way we feel in these spaces.

It is therefore important to note that for every imaginable use, new requirements arise and normative standards take effect, which can restrict our plans and goals. Furthermore, prevailing circumstances may vary from case to case. Consequently, adopting a general categorical approach to light planning is very difficult; normally, individual planning will be required in every case.

Whereas historical light planning was primarily concerned with introducing daylight into interior spaces, illuminating predetermined areas with sunlight at certain times of the day, and ensuring that night illumination was available with natural sources of light, contemporary lighting design can offer a far greater choice of variations and technical options. At the same time, demands are constantly growing. Guidelines have to be followed and minimum and maximum values complied with. Human sensitivities adapt to new lighting situations, and, last but not least, the energy efficiency of artificial light and sunlight need to be taken into consideration. As a result, the complexity of planning tasks has increased in the field of interior planning and architecture, resulting in an ever higher degree of specialization in the domain of lighting design. The Development of Lighting Design

The Foundations of Lighting Design

The question of how we employ naturally available as well as artificially added light raises certain design issues that need to be clarified in advance: which specifications does a particular light source fulfil or have to fulfil, and which measurable values are available. Above all, and as far as planning specifications are concerned, the physical properties must be addressed, since they form a crucial part of the planning background. Furthermore, it is necessary, as far as the actual planning is concerned, to establish which properties are to be utilized. Moreover, it is essential to identify which tasks the light has to perform. In addition, certain specifications may have to be met with regard to basic lighting, as well as room and accent lighting, which may differ quite considerably, or have to be achieved through a variety of means.

THE PLANNING PROCESS

The individual stages of light planning are barely distinguishable from the standard sequences of architectural planning. The fundamental data, as well as the design and its execution, define the process. During the first stage, the client or user specifies the desired functions and defines, above all, the areas to be illuminated and the specific colour scheme required. In the draft stage, the components are primarily considered from the standpoint of artificial lighting, such as the types of lighting and illuminants, since the daylight components are — in the case of pure lighting design — generally defined by the position, size and style of the windows. The components and furnishings are then put in position. To this end, computer-aided simulations can be generated — when required or desired — that reflect the room's spatial effect. These simulations cannot, however, serve as a substitute for sampling individual components in a specific installation context, for only here can the individual installation situation be chosen definitively. Interaction between light planners and electronics planners is essential, since the cable routes and the positioning of the switches must also be considered.   ○

○ **Note:** Owing to the growing opportunities in computer-aided design, many situations in the planning process can now be illustrated, as in the case of rendering, illumination scenarios, calculations, etc. These are not, however, a substitute for sampling or for reexamining work on the spot, because the individual's perception of a light situation cannot be simulated down to the very last detail – despite photorealistic renderings.

PHYSICS TERMINOLOGY AND PARAMETERS

Owing to light's complexity, many different parameters are used to describe and do justice to the various aspects of this subject. > Tab. 1

The light and colour spectrum

To the human eye, only a minuscule part of the electromagnetic spectrum is perceptible. This field is known as the light or colour spectrum. It is also frequently referred to as real "light". Higher-frequency ranges with short wavelengths (such as UV or X-rays) and low-frequency ranges with long wavelengths (microwaves and radio waves) are invisible to the human eye. Within the range of the visible light spectrum, it is possible to determine the diverse wavelengths of the colour tones. > Tab. 2

Luminous flux, luminous efficacy and the quantity of light

Luminous flux Φ [lm] shows how much light is radiated from a light source. In order to establish this fact, the human eye is needed as an evaluating organ. When calculating the luminous efficacy, the quantity of light, the light yield and the luminance, it is essential to regard luminous

Tab. 1: An overview of the photometrical parameters

Parameter	Symbol	Unit
Luminous flux	Φ	lumen [lm]
Luminous efficacy	η	lumens per watt [lm/W]
Luminous energy	Q	lumen seconds [lms]
Light yield	I	candela [cd]
Illuminance	E	lux [lx]
Daylight factor	D	percentage [%]
Light density	L	candela per m² [cd/m²]
Colour temperature	–	Kelvin [K]
Colour rendering index	R_a	–

Tab. 2: The wavelengths of the colours of the spectrum

Hue	Wavelength [nm]
Red	710–630
Orange	630–580
Yellow	580–560
Green	560–480
Blue	480–420
Violet	420–380

flux as a baseline value. In the case of artificial light sources, the luminous flux levels used for the <u>light calculations</u> are stated — depending on the product — by the manufacturers. In order to balance the energy and perform investment appraisals, it is necessary to calculate the <u>luminous efficacy η</u> [lm/W] — an essential source of light. This, in turn, calculates the energy required to reach the nominal value. <u>The quantity of light Q</u> [lm × h] states the entire luminous flux emitted by a light source over a defined period of time. A light source with highly concentrated luminous flux thus produces a greater quantity of light per unit than a light source containing very little luminous flux.

<u>Light yield I</u> [cd] determines the ratio of light emitted by a light source moving in a certain direction. The luminous intensity of natural light sources can be influenced by the use not only of sun-shade and glare protection, but also of glazing and light control. In the case of artificial light, these are the essential light models and light sources/illuminants used. > Fig. 1

Light yield

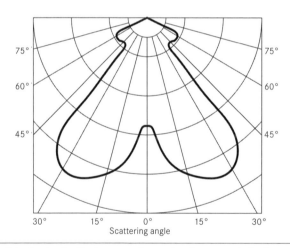

Fig. 1: The light density distribution curve of a rotationally symmetrical reflector

In the case of <u>illuminance E</u> [lx; lm/m²], the luminous flux represents a specific illuminated area. Above all, when illuminating workplaces, extensive normative specifications apply that determine which values are reached, or should not be exceeded. In the case of daylight design, the decisive values are generally the readily available illumination intensities of natural light sources; when planning artificial lighting, calculations should be made and simulation models calculated to ascertain which lights and illuminants will be needed to produce the necessary illumination intensity. > Tab. 3

The <u>daylight factor quotient D</u> describes the relationship between a room's illumination intensity (the centre of the room) and illumination intensities outside and beneath a cloudy sky. In both cases, the quotient is always derived from specific measurements and/or detailed calculations. In both cases, a pattern of grids containing a number of points can be laid out in the rooms observed in order to arrive at a distinct surface display. This makes sense in rooms that are exposed to natural lighting from different directions.

$$D = \frac{E_{interior}}{E_{exterior}} \times 100$$

D — Daylight factor [%]

$E_{interior}$ — Lighting intensity interior [lx]

$E_{exterior}$ — Lighting intensity exterior [lx]

Tab. 3: The illumination intensities of natural light sources on the ground

Light source	Luminance [lx]
Clear sky, sunny (summer)	90,000–130,000
Clear sky, sunny (winter)	19,000–25,000
Cloudy sky (summer)	15,000–20,000
Cloudy sky (winter)	5,000–8,000
Dusk	3–750
Moonlight	0.02–0.30

○ **Note:** Tables and values on specific parameters can often be found in the norms and guidelines. When reading the set values, please note that quite different demands are shown for both the minimum and medium illumination intensities, as well as for the horizontal and vertical areas.

Light density is the parameter within physics that describes the brightness experienced by human beings. It is one of the few units that is extremely dependent on the direction of a source of light. Hence, luminance is always dependent on a generator and not — as in the case of most other parameters — on the recipient of the light radiation, i.e., the human eye. Furthermore, the awareness of darkness and glare through the perception of diverse sensitivities of the eye varies according to the eye's sensitivity. Not only that: the eye adapts itself to certain situations over the course of time. In addition, the wavelengths of light, that is, the perceived colour, ensure that similar light densities trigger differentiated feelings. > Tab. 4

Luminous colour or colour temperature (unit of measure: Kelvin) describes a colour impression produced by a light source. A lower value alludes to a large share of red in the existing colour spectrum, in which subjective perception is experienced as warm. Above all, in the planning of the temperature, the colour plays a major role in determining the artificial light sources, since the planning goal generally is to simulate natural light. The technical capabilities, however, generally end with colour temperatures well below those of natural light. > Tab. 5 Light sources with a colour temperature of under 3,300 K are registered as warm-white, and have a neutral white spectrum fluctuating between 3,300 and 5,000 K; higher values result in warm "daylight white" or "cold white" light sources.

The colour rendering index R_a serves to display the quality of the colour rendering of diverse light sources. In the process, it describes the impact evoked by light directed at objects and other people. Good colour renditioning is achieved when a natural colour environment is optimally reproduced (value $R_a = 100$). In high-quality interiors with good residential quality and/or workplaces with light sources, an $R_a < 80$ should not be used. > Tab. 6 The colour rendering index R_a refers to the eight most frequently used test colours. The index makes this quite clear and means in this context: "in general".

Tab. 4: The perception and sensitivity of the human eye

Viewing task	Light density
Night vision	3–30 μcd/m² – 3–30 mcd/m²
Twilight	3–30 mcd/m² – 3–30 cd/m²
Daylight	> 3–30 cd/m²
Dazzle	> 100,000–1,000,000 cd/m²

Tab. 5: Exemplary colour temperatures of natural and artificial sources of light

The source of light	Colour temperature [K]
Candle	1,500
Light bulb (60 W)	2,700
Light bulb (200 W)	3,000
Halogen lamp (12 V)	3,000–3,200
Fluorescent lamp (neutral white)	4,000
Morning/evening sun	5,000
Cloudy sky	6,500–7,500
Fog/haze	7,500–8,500
Clear sky	9,000–12,000

Tab. 6: Colour reproduction index with diverse light sources

Source of light	Colour rendering index R_a
Light bulb	Up to 100
LED	80–97
OLED	80–90
Fluorescent lamp	50–98
Metal halide lamp	60–95
High-pressure sodium lamp	18–85
High-pressure quicksilver lamp	45
Low-pressure sodium vapour lamp	< 44

ILLUMINATION TASKS

Planning with lamps and illumination basically calls for a holistic approach to many different types of illumination. Initially, the general lighting (or basic illumination) is intended to ensure uniform illumination for a predefined area. Accent lighting is more differentiated in the next step, because it means creating – within what are now generally illuminated area zones – a foreground and background. In addition to this, special points of emphasis and accentuated surfaces can be created.

Lighting in general   General lighting is planned with the aim of ensuring equally good orientation in all parts of a room. It fulfils the basic task of making things visible and ensures that the room is perceived in this way. > Fig. 2 Since primarily diffuse sources of light are used here to create or minimize contrasts, for example by casting shadows or directing the light rays in a

Fig. 2: Overall lighting/illumination in a living room and a conference room

Fig. 3: Examples of the accentuated lighting of objects and room zones

certain manner, an exclusive form of general lighting will not suffice in most cases to emphasize the room's function or highlight the activities of the person inside the room. To this end, more ambitious steps must be taken. All-purpose lighting is planned so that it can still be used even if there is a change in functions or use.

The accentuation or arrangement of light sources on specific zones or objects is referred to as accentuated illumination. In this case, contrasts are created that – due to the general lighting – do not have a sufficient impact, as yet. > Fig. 3 Here, illumination systems are used that direct or bundle daylight or, in the case of artificial light sources, rely on narrow beams and adjustable lamps. In order to illuminate and stage the surfaces, a combination of the brightness from the lamps and the emerging shadows is used to emphasize the structure, the colouring and the

Accentuated illumination and the illumination of surfaces

Fig. 4: Examples of the illumination of surfaces

materiality. To this end, lights are often used that are not directed straight
● at the surface, but appear as scattered light or rays of light. > Fig. 4

The illumination of interior and outside spaces

The tasks of lighting design differ from those of urban lighting design, and frequently extend to the illumination of a single object in a display case. The catalogue of requirements encompasses – in the case of
all plans – the general situation with regard to interior and exterior space,
the use of space and rooms, the desired and required illumination, as
well as its useful life. Consequently, a concept needs to be developed
that takes into account the amounts of daylight and artificial light, the
types of artificial lighting and the existing buildings, as well as objects
and surfaces. In the following, the available planning elements will be
presented and an overview of the potential areas of use for diverse plan-
○ ning scenarios underlined.

● **Example:** In the case of street lighting, equipping a
street area with an adequate number of street lamps
at regular intervals will ensure a sufficient amount of
lighting. The siting of a large number of lamps at or
near crossroads, and using reflecting signs at danger
spots, will make the latter stand out and encourage
people to pay greater attention to these zones.

○ **Note:** The growing significance of light planning can
also be seen in the fact that urban authorities are
increasingly developing light concepts that define the
functionality and design of light in open space. The goal
of these concepts, which are now obligatory up to a
certain point, is to create a harmonic overall impression of urban lighting.

Planning elements

DAYLIGHT

The use of natural sunlight and night light is one of the core tasks as far as the planning and illumination of interior and exterior spaces is concerned. As an exclusive light source, or as a light source supported by artificial light > Chapter Artificial Light, it is the task of light planners to ensure that there is a user-specific degree of light available for end users. In many cases, such as secretarial work with screens and monitors, a certain degree of glare-protection light is essential; this can be provided through glare protection or light guidance. In the case of daylight planning, it is almost equally important in most naturally illuminated rooms to keep an eye on thermal insulation, which makes sun protection measures necessary, depending on which way the room is facing. The overall concept of light planning ought to have as its goal the minimal employment of artificial light in order to create the required degree of brightness.

Daylight is subject to natural fluctuations. In this regard, both the temporal aspects (the time of day, a specific season), which determine, above all, the angle of incidence and the refraction of daylight, as well as superordinate and subordinate local issues play a role. The superordinate aspects cannot be influenced by the planners, or only to a minor degree: the latitude and longitude of the location, the topography, the distance and height of the surrounding buildings/vegetation. The subordinate points can be influenced during the design and planning stages (the alignment of buildings and spaces, as well as rooms and exposure areas). ○

The use of daylight in interiors

The use of daylight in interior spaces has a considerable impact on people's well-being. The human organism adapts to the daily disappearance and return of natural light; this process controls not only our sleeping-waking rhythm, but also the release of hormones and the operation

○ **Note:** When planning the alignment of buildings and the resulting irradiation factors, a solar altitude diagram can be consulted that shows the day and year in which certain dependent values are stated. (> Fig. 5) These values are cited in DIN 5034-2 for this core region of Germany.

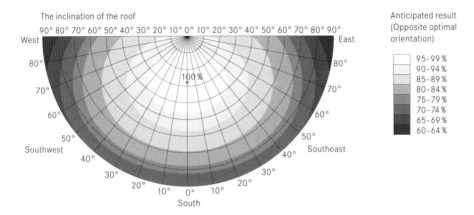

The inclinication of the roof

90° 80° 70° 60° 50° 40° 30° 20° 10° 0° 10° 20° 30° 40° 50° 60° 70° 80° 90°

West — East

Southwest

Southeast

South

Anticipated result
(Opposite optimal
orientation)

- 95–99 %
- 90–94 %
- 85–89 %
- 80–84 %
- 75–79 %
- 70–74 %
- 65–69 %
- 60–64 %

Fig. 5: An exemplary sun chart

of our metabolic functions. This rhythm, which is linked to the presence or absence of sunlight, not only controls our general perceptions but also has an influence on our physical and psychological health. The human eye also evaluates certain light situations.

Thanks to this connection, the inclusion of daylight in lighting design has a positive effect on those who want to use space. From an energy standpoint too, the use of natural light is advantageous, because every time a source of artificial light is used, additional electrical energy is required. The sun's light also reaches colour temperatures that are agreeable to human beings, but very difficult, if not impossible, to reproduce with the means of artificial light.

The aforementioned problems encountered by light planners (the limited natural daylight available during the course of the day, seasonal irregularities, etc.) necessitate complex solutions. Measures are taken to guide and control delivery of light in order to prevent a light fall-off in the depths of the room, to avoid glare and to regulate heat input. In the planning phase, it is important to focus on the ways the space will be utilized, as workplaces, in particular, present normative challenges that can hardly be dealt with by the use of sunlight alone.

Planning elements for daylight use

Daylight design involves diverse methods of making natural light available. As far as outside areas are concerned, this is generally a question of restricting irradiation in order to avoid glare, whereas for interior rooms it is a matter of providing protection from the sun. Consequently, precise analyses of interior rooms must be carried out with regard to the creation of daylight apertures.

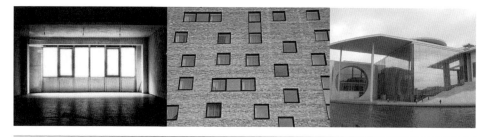

Fig. 6: Diverse windows and types

An obvious way to supply rooms with daylight is to create openings in the room-encompassing shell. The windows' size, position, partitioning and materials influence how it is possible — despite the windows — to allow only an essential amount of light into interior rooms in order to avoid glare or an excessive generation of heat. As far as daylight design is concerned, the window is the element that offers the greatest variation. It is also the one that has to fulfil the most demands:

— Size
   In contemporary architecture, windows can be made to almost any size. With some constructive effort, facades and roofs can be designed with the greatest degree of transparency. Large window areas, however, also place greater demands on statics, solar protection and thermal protection.

— Form
   In window design, many variations are possible. Round and trapeze-shaped windows can be realized, as well as arching elements and wide ribbon windows with countless individual windows arranged alongside one another. > Fig. 6

— The position and arrangement
   Both the window's position within the building's shell (in the outer wall, cellar, or roof, as a skylight, or in an interior courtyard) and its positioning within the assigned room (the middle of the room, for example, or a corner) must be taken into account. Furthermore, the window can be located in a specific part of the building and positioned in the reveal (exterior, interior, glass curtain wall). > Fig. 7

Fig. 7: The fenestration in the inner courtyard, the corner of the building, and the skylight

Fig. 8: Windows with diverse glass/frame elements and sash windows

— The relationship of the glass, the frame and the distribution of the windows

The following basic principle applies here: the larger the window, the greater the share of glass in relation to the frame profile. With additional steps, rungs and bolts, a creative or structural distribution can be achieved. > Fig. 8

— Materials made of glass and frames

Glass plays a very special role in antiglare and solar protection measures, as well as in heat protection. Clear glass ensures intense lighting, as well as high heat input. With the aid of colour dyes, the light input can be reduced, and with the aid of multiple glazing the insulation properties can be improved. In the case of frame constructions, wood, artificial materials and metals (such as aluminium and steel), or a combination of these, can be installed.

In addition to introducing direct daylight via apertures in the outer Indirect systems shell, indirect systems of <u>light control</u> and <u>guidance</u> ensure a well-moderated, scattered or channelled incident light. Daylight is primarily regulated outside or inside window levels by directly reflecting or scattering sunlight. In this case, standard systems employing lamellas and shutters can be used, which also perform the function of solar protection. Alternatively, light-guiding glass can be used, in which the cavity between the glass panels plays a key role as a light reflector. In order to bridge greater distances in longer rooms, additional light-guiding measures must be undertaken. These do not necessarily have to be structurally complicated or expensive solutions, such as light wells, light pipes or solar lamps > Fig. 9, which usually tend to be overly complicated or technically unfeasible. By carefully selecting not only the appropriate surface structures for the interior walls and ceilings, as well as coats of light paint with a highly reflective quality, even an unfavourably designed ground plan can be supplied with sufficient daylight.

O

In the case of natural indirect lighting, where interior rooms have no direct contact with the outside world, such as corridors in office buildings, <u>translucent elements can be built into the walls and doors</u>. Here, as in the case of window glazing, clear and toned glass, as well as translucent glass elements can be used. Only in rare cases, however, is this type of illumination satisfactory. With regard to mobility and access, as well as for safety reasons (escape routes, safety lighting), permanent artificial lighting is advisable.

Light management for daylight design always raises technical issues. Light management Generally speaking, light management also involves connecting a room's artificial illumination sources. With the aid of a daylight-dependent lighting control system, such as a DALI control (Digital Addressable Lighting Interface), an independently operating system can be used to support or

> O **Note:** A major disadvantage of light-guiding systems is that they only function in direct sunlight; diffuse sky light (under a cloudy sky) cannot be passed on. This is particularly problematic when the sun is not shining, since that is when the need for light in interior rooms is greatest. Hence, a location must be chosen in which an indirect system can be meaningfully employed. In Central Europe, for instance, sunny hours account for 45 to 60 % of the total.

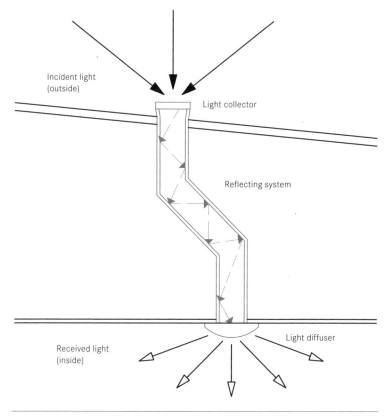

Incident light
(outside)

Light collector

Reflecting system

Received light
(inside)

Light diffuser

Fig. 9: The functional principle behind the light flue and the light pipe

replace a manual light management system (using switches and dimmers), by following (or replacing) appropriately programmed rules. Data is collected on the room lighting/brightness via sensors, which — on reaching certain thresholds — switch the room lighting on or off. Lighting <u>control systems</u> of this nature are generally used in offices and commercial businesses, since their light scenarios are pre-programmed and assignable to specific scenarios and illumination groups. These types of control systems, however, are frequently installed in private contexts. The DALI lighting system can be used in conjunction with certain interfaces (Bus-systems; EIB (Europe)/LON (USA)), and also integrated into a superordinate, household building management system, in which solar protection, air-conditioning systems, air-conditioning technology, heating and cooling are controlled independently of one another. > Fig. 10

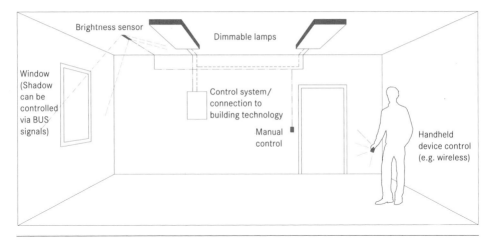

Fig. 10: An exemplary construction of a DALI-control system

Solar protection and antiglare protection

External factors, such as neighbourhood development, vegetation, the form of a building and the location of a room within a building, can result in a reduction and moderation of light in the area to be planned. If, however, these measures are not enough to sufficiently contain the light and heat input, additional systems for providing sun and glare protection will have to be provided. Diverse systems can be positioned in front of the facade or window, on the inside or at window level. There may also be a desire to block out the sun completely, to deflect its rays, or to filter a certain amount of its light. Ideally, the system should be individually regulating; in other words, it ought, if necessary, to be adapted to diverse requirements internally and to the weather situation externally, have an appropriate ventilation system (even when it is "shut down"), and be easy to use. Last but not least, economic and design considerations should be taken into account.

From the standpoint of heating, external systems are the most useful since they capture the sun's rays before these reach a window element, thus preventing the elements in the facade from overheating. Systems such as <u>shutters</u> and <u>daylight control systems</u> use rigid or mobile horizontal lamellas, which either deflect or irradiate a user-optimized share of the radiation. With reflecting or matte lamellas, it is possible to manipulate the share of irradiation by redirecting it or fading it out. One great advantage is that — depending on the sun's position in the sky — one can reduce the direct radiation while at the same time preserving a view of the surroundings.

External structures

Fig. 11: External venetian blinds in laminated metal

Fig. 12: Canopies designed to shade the window elements

Awnings operate on the principle that the formation of shadows on the facade opening prevents or limits irradiation. Awnings, too, can generally be rolled in and out (roll-up and folding awnings) and provide additional protection from the weather. The materials used — mainly synthetic fibres such as acrylic or polyester, enriched with variously coloured dyes — determine the degree of radiation and translucence.

As with all external structures, wind susceptibility increases the need for cleaning. Furthermore, lamella structures have to be monitored to establish the effects of the wind. Frequently, therefore, wind sensors are fixed to the facade, because any transgression of predefined limits would
○ automatically cause the shutters and awnings to retract.

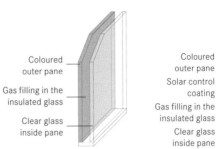

Coloured outer pane

Gas filling in the insulated glass

Clear glass inside pane

Coloured outer pane

Solar control coating

Gas filling in the insulated glass

Clear glass inside pane

Fig. 13: Interior glare protection provided by fully or partially pleated blinds

Fig. 14: Examples: Coated glazing/dyed glazing

The systems installed in the interior often consist of blinds – or roller blinds – assembled immediately before glazing. > Fig. 13 Standard curtains and drapes provide antiglare protection and, in some cases, a certain diffusion of light. As in the case of awnings, they allow for a choice of materials and colours. Easy accessibility, cleaning, and mounting give them a distinct advantage over outside elements. Often, interiors and exteriors are combined in order to gain the greatest degree of individual adaptation to the desired light situation.

Interior constructions

The most common variation consisting of glazed window elements (and one that limits the sun's radiation inside rooms and buildings) is that of <u>solar control glazing</u>. The manufacture of anti-sun glass involves a dying process in which a part of the radiating sun's energy is absorbed, whereas the process of coating the glass (generally using multi-sheet windows on the inside of the external pane) results in a reflection of the sun's radiation. > Fig. 14 Solar control glazing makes it possible to keep the

Glazing

○ **Note:** This applies to sun sensors too, which, in case of excessive energy inputs, shut down the sun-shading elements, thereby creating an undesirable situation for light planners. Hence, in certain cases, and despite the lack of sunlight, venetian blinds have to be lowered. Circumstances of this nature must be taken into consideration during the planning phase.

Fig. 15: Examples of milk glass and capillary glass

○ sun's radiation level at around 50 to 80%; the manufacturer's own estimation is represented by the g-value of the respective glazing process.

If, in addition to ensuring overall protection from the sun, the aim is to avoid being able to see through the glazing without, however, entirely restricting the transport of light, <u>frosted glass</u>, or <u>translucent panes of glass</u>, are generally used. In this case, etching techniques, screen printing, sandblasting, diverse coatings, and foiling allow for a variety of designs. If a very high spread of entering light is to be achieved, <u>capillary glass</u> can be used as an interesting – albeit costly – design variation. In this case, a <u>translucent glass</u> solution offering thermal insulation based on a fabric with hollow cavities has been employed, ensuring a higher degree of transmission of the overall construction.

○ **Note:** The g-value indicates the overall amount of escaping energy of the total solar energy transmittance of the antiglare protection, or, in other words, both the direct transmission share of the sun's energy as well as the share of energy in the radiation and heat transfer, which is transferred – via the glazing – to the room. A low g-value indicates a high degree of solar protection. Sun-protection glasses generally have a g-value of 0.3 to 0.5, which means that 30 to 50% of the sun's energy has reached the internal space. Nowadays, high-grade glasses can be manufactured with a g-value as low as 0.15.

Fig. 16: Double-shell facade profile construction with interior, translucent insulation

Fig. 17: An example of deactivated/activated switchable glazing

Profile glass is a special type of translucent glass. The latter is manufactured in a U-form cast, making it particularly stable and relatively easy
to produce at considerable construction heights. In addition to its use as
a light-diffusing element in a facade aperture, it is also frequently chosen
for facade cladding. As a double-shell element used in connection with
translucent insulation material, it can also be employed as a non-bearing
external wall element. > Fig. 16

Switchable glasses reduce the sun's light and glare — and especially
its heat input — by changing or blurring the colour with the aid of an electrical or thermal impulse. In contrast to sun-protection glasses, which
are permanently coloured, switchable glasses are clear in a non-activated
state. Since diverse variants are still in the development phase, or in a
very expensive stage of manufacture, they are seldom employed in hous-
ing projects and office buildings. > Fig. 17

ARTIFICIAL LIGHT

In interior rooms, artificial light sources are often the only types, and they are highly sought after owing to the great diversity of light colours they offer and the wealth of opportunities for adjustment, control and modelling. However, people often find it difficult to remain for long in rooms equipped exclusively with artificial light. Artificial lighting can emphasize a room's use by designing and creating focal centres, or by deliberately changing and manipulating a familiar situation. In contrast to daylight, artificial lighting is available for long stretches of time.

Economic factors and environmental criteria also play an important role in the use of artificial lighting. With the aid of refraction and by simulating light, the distribution of light and light quantities must be calculated in exactly the same way as the consumption of electricity and sustainability (maintenance and disposal) in order to compare the costs and uses. Furthermore, there are comprehensive standards and guidelines on the varying uses of light, which the planners have to deal with.

Planning elements for the use of artificial light

Artificial sources of light

Artificial light sources produce light by supplying electrical current. Great diversity with regard to requirements has led to the appearance of a wide variety of illuminants, which can be used for many purposes.

Thermal radiator

Sources that generate light via hot filaments are referred to as thermal radiators. > Fig. 18 In terms of energy, however, electric light bulbs and halogen lamps are not very efficient in comparison with other sources of lighting, because their luminous efficiency and lifetimes are very short. Thermal radiators, nevertheless, are counted among those sources whose light we find warm and generally experience as pleasant. Their light also resembles white light, in the absence of natural light. If an area is partially lit by daylight, however, and a light bulb glows, the yellow colour's impact will be far greater than that of the sunlight. The classic standard light bulb, which is no longer bought and sold in shops, forms the basis of all artificial-light planning and the development of modern lamps.

Discharge lamps

Discharge lamps generate light by guiding electrical current through a gas contained in a sealed, illuminating body. > Fig. 19 A distinction is made with regard to the pressure between high-pressure discharge lamps (halogen-metal halide lamps, high-pressure sodium lamps and mercury vapour lamps) and low-pressure discharge lamps (induction lamps, fluorescent/low-pressure lamps and low-pressure sodium vapour lamps). Low-pressure sodium vapour lamps in particular are distinguished by the fact that they — as thermal radiators –have a far greater life expectancy. As they emit a comparable quantity of light, their energy requirement is much lower. On the other hand, discharge lamps are quite limited with

Fig. 18: Thermal radiators — standard light bulbs and halogen lamps

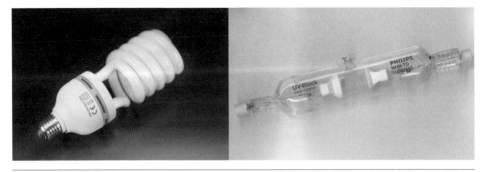

Fig. 19: Examples of discharge lamps

regard to their colour reproduction. Whereas low-pressure discharge lamps — especially those in the form of the neon tube — are very frequently used in the non-private sphere, high-pressure discharge lamps are generally used in streets and for industrial lighting.

In the case of electroluminescent lamps, radiation is generated by a build-up of voltage and electricity on a semi-conductor, yet without releasing any thermal energy as is the case with thermal radiators. In the process, the light source radiates constant brightness in all directions. The most commonly used form is the light-emitting diode (LED), which is able, by filtering or selecting the semiconductor, to reproduce the various colour tones. LED lamps, manufactured in the form of a standard light bulb, have meanwhile replaced the classic light bulb and are manufactured with the same sockets and screw threads. > Fig. 20 The higher price of materials is offset by the far longer life and equal distribution of

Electroluminescent lamps

light. Special forms such as <u>organic light-emitting diodes (OLED)</u> and <u>electroluminescent displays</u> have primarily found their use in computer and monitor technology. They are characterized by their great flexibility, while their luminous flux and luminance are far lower than that of standard LEDs. In the domain of architectonic light planning, their main use is for rooms designed to provide light uniformly and two-dimensionally.

Lamps   A fixture that serves to house light sources is referred to as a lamp. Lamps are not generally designed for just one type of illumination or one specific illuminant, but are able to use various sockets and connections, depending on the lamp concerned. The products are categorized in line with the type of product and assembly. Owing to increasingly differentiated demands, requirements and designs, manufacturers nowadays combine most types of lamps — depending on the form and design — in individual ranges.

Outside lighting   As far as outdoor use is concerned, very diverse designs in both the private (garden and path lighting) and public domain are being produced. For public functions such as street and path lighting, light columns (lanterns) are mostly used, which are spanned above the street or pathway on pendant luminaires. > Fig. 21 They are also used privately as wall luminaires for entrance lighting and as radiators to accentuate house facades.

Parks and public spaces offer considerable opportunity for experimentation. Illuminated and self-lighting stelas, bollard luminaires, as well as adaptable lamps are used just as much as floor and wall lamps dug into the ground, bollard luminaires (adjustable), and projectors, as well as variants built into plinths and steps. > Fig. 22

○ **Note:** Due to their ever-greater use, external lamps designed for the public sphere are now being manufactured to make them vandal-safe. This is done by using more stable materials for the boundaries and mounts, as well as unbreakable covers for the lamps. Nevertheless, no one can guarantee these materials against deliberate acts of destruction.

Fig. 20: Examples of electroluminescent lamps

Fig. 21: Examples of mast lights and hanging lamps

Fig. 22: Bollard lighting, recessed luminaires and illuminated stairs in the public domain

Tab. 7: IP – ways of protecting lamps according to BS EN 60529

Protection from foreign bodies/touch protection		Protection from the effects of water	
Code	Protection class	Code	Protection class
0	Not protected	0	Not protected
1	Protection against solid foreign bodies > 50 mm, protection against extensive touching.	1	Protection against dripping water.
2	Protection against solid foreign bodies > 12 mm, protection from touching with one's finger.	2	Protection against dripping water (below 15° deviation from the perpendicular).
3	Protection against solid foreign bodies > 2.5 mm, protection against being touched with tools, wire, etc.	3	Protection against dripping water (below 60° deviation from the vertical).
4	Protection against solid foreign bodies > 1 mm, protection against being touched with tools, wire, etc.	4	Protection against splashing water.
5	Protection from dust, fully protected against touching under tension.	5	Protected against water out of a nozzle.
6	Protected from dust, fully protected against touching under tension.	6	Protected against heavy sea.
		7	Protected against the consequences of immersion.
		8	Protected against continuous immersion.

When choosing an appropriate external lamp, attention has to be paid to the protection type required. The type defines the degree to which a luminaire is protected against external impact (mechanically and from water). This information is derived from the designation "IP", and from two consecutive numbers. > Tab. 7

Ceiling lamps The most frequently used type of lamp in both the private and commercial spheres is the louvre luminaire, which often permits free positioning and allocation to specific functions and areas of use. If the lamps are attached flush to a suspended ceiling, for example, they are referred to as recessed luminaires. A specific form of lamp, fixed to the ceiling, is the raster luminaire. Within the framework of a grid ceiling system, the raster luminaire replaces single ceiling elements and can even form the ceiling itself. In contrast to fitted lamps, those mounted directly onto the ceiling with visible luminary are referred to as surface-mounted luminaires. Surface-mounted ceiling systems come in all imaginable forms and colours. > Fig. 23 They not only serve as a pure source of light but have also become an integral part of architectonic design. Another special form of ceiling lamp is the pendant luminaire, or suspended lamp. This solitary lamp, which is also hung in rows from the ceiling, is used to

Fig. 23: Examples of ceiling lamps

Fig. 24: Examples of wall lamps

lend emphasis to a specific area. In rooms with high ceilings, such as multi-story foyers and halls, it is also used to prevent light from spreading too far. In private apartments, lamps of this type are generally hung above the dining table; in offices they are hung above tables or in conference and discussion rooms. Owing to their position inside the room, pendant lamps can illuminate both the areas beneath the luminaires, and the ceiling area if the selected product allows light to escape upwards.

Wall lamps are used in interiors to supplement basic illumination in otherwise insufficiently lit rooms, or to accentuate lighting in areas that require special emphasis. Radiation is generally directed upward and/or downward; direct rays of light are usually avoided. Externally, directly radiated light is used more frequently. > Fig. 24

Wall lighting

Fig. 25: Examples of standing lamps

Fig. 26: Examples of table and desk lamps

Standing lamps — For reasons of flexibility, standing lamps are designed for private use or in offices where they are not assigned to any particular place. Depending on the room's use or allocation, lamps can be positioned anywhere. In existing buildings with low ceilings, where suspended ceilings or ceiling surface-mounted luminaires cannot be used, standing lamps also serve as an ideal alternative. > Fig. 25

Table lamps — Similar to standing lamps, but smaller and more flexible in format, table lamps are used as freely positionable illumination. The desk lamp is a typical example. Nowadays, table lamps and standing lamps are sometimes equipped with built-in sensors and automatic dimmer functions. > Fig. 26

Standard illumination control systems are by no means restricted to Lighting control systems the standard light switch, which can, at best, only be supplemented by additional dimmers. Depending on the lamps and illuminants, electronic control equipment, transformers, and/or manual releases may be required and have to be taken into consideration in household planning. Furthermore, integration into the building's overall technology is necessary if interaction with artificial lighting systems and other functions is envisaged, such as house intelligent building technology, or an optimized daytime and artificial-lighting mixing system is desired.

■

The positioning of the controlling elements (sensors, detectors, etc.), the controlled elements (lighting, solar protection, ventilation, etc.), and the types of controllers are meanwhile very diversified. Types of control include time-based control systems, which also operate through pre-programming, as well as motion sensors, controlled on-off switches, and light-dependent systems. With the aid of external sensors, they regulate the illumination times and illumination intensities in the interior (luminous intensity).

■ **Tip:** An important and, unfortunately, frequently neglected aspect of planning is the expedient positioning of switches and other control elements. In many instances – and not only in the case of constructions, conversions and the redevelopment of existing buildings – light switches have been found behind doors or in inaccessible places.

Planning scenarios

The goal of light planning is to use the planning elements – daylight and artificial light – in a meaningful way for the planning task at hand and to combine them. There are many different public and private fields of application, each of which uses specific elements that are appropriate and others which – for technical and design reasons from the standpoint of design – should not be used.

STREET LIGHTING AND EXTERNAL LIGHTING

The main task of street lighting is to ensure the safety of road users. The basis of planning lies in values that constitute the norms and guidelines which are to be applied – especially in the presence of pedestrians. The essential elements of standard illumination are loadbearing systems, housings, ballast, ballast units and ignitions, light-guiding systems (mirrors) and sources of lighting. The most common of these is the "lantern", with a ballast unit made of fibre-reinforced composite synthetic material. > Fig. 27 An operating device for upstream installation or ignition is necessary because it uses sodium vapour, mercury vapour and fluorescent lamps as an illuminant. In contemporary street lighting, high-pressure sodium-vapour lamps/LED lamps are now being used with ever greater frequency. The use of high-pressure sodium-vapour lamps is still the most economical choice, since they not only have a very long lifetime but also a far more compact design than low-pressure lamps.

In general, street lighting is switched on and off via a central control that triggers the switching procedure following a time signal, or by brightness sensors that trigger the switching procedure at dusk.

Car park lighting and parking lots   In principle, the above-mentioned modes of street illumination can also be used in car parks if they are located outside. > Fig. 28 Here, too, the light column remains the most common type. The height of the light source has to be adapted to the size of the car park. In the case of small parking lots, structures of up to 4.50 m in height make sense. With larger parking spaces, they may be as high as 12 m. The lighting should not be manipulated, but radiate horizontally to achieve an equal distribution of light over the entire area. The same benchmark should apply to all parking areas > Tab. 8 in order to ensure a general sense of security, and to make sure that the faces of approaching people can be recognized.

Fig. 27: Examples of street and exterior lighting

Fig. 28: Examples of parking lot lighting

Tab. 8: The required lighting level for parking spaces and multi-story car parks

Area	Luminance [lx]
Parking lot (outside) (semi-cylindrical illuminance)	1.5–5
Multi-story car parks / car park	10
Carports / parking spaces (medium illumination strength)	75
Entries and exits (daytime)	300
Entries and exits (nighttime)	75

○ **Note:** Benchmarks must be established for the overall lighting of parking lots, which can be measured at any given point within the space. For security's sake, the necessary illumination intensity refers to a semi-cylindrical area to the height of 1.50 m, in which a face turned toward the observer is identifiable.

Fig. 29: Examples of lighting for underground car parks and multi-story car parks

In the case of multi-story car parks, and especially underground garages, planning is far more complicated. In addition to overall illumination, the illumination of the driveways, the entrances and exits, the parking spaces and pedestrian routing has to be considered. In order to respond to the eye's need to adapt to modified illumination when entering and leaving the car park, transitional areas with varying illumination intensities for day and night operation are necessary. > Fig. 29

The illumination of parks and squares

Apart from the overall need for powerful lighting to ensure public safety, it is difficult to make general statements regarding the illumination of parks and public squares. Indeed, very few universally valid comments have been made regarding the design of such spaces. There are, for instance, a number of individual scenarios related to the environment, the use of the park and the volume of traffic. For example, not only the square itself, but also the surrounding buildings, can be illuminated and serve as a source of light. Apart from illuminating pathways, certain aesthetic objects can be singled out not only by lighting, but also by certain types of colouring. > Fig. 30

In order to gain the necessary illumination capacity, street mast luminaires are frequently employed, provided there is sufficient space to obtain the necessary illumination intensities for general lighting. In this case, column luminaires can be used to obtain the required illumination intensity for general lighting, and assuming there is sufficient capacity. If required, these can be supplemented not only by bollard luminaires, but also by installing and mounting lights in floors, wall areas and stairs in order to brighten up the areas used by people. To achieve the anticipated impact, it is very important to use lamps with a suitable protection class.

Fig. 30: Examples of illuminating public spaces

PUBLIC BUILDINGS

If areas are publicly accessible, the needs of many different people will have to be taken into account. Among other things, illumination designs must support people with diminished sight. Diverse usages and types can also create various expectations, which must be fulfilled by the light design.

Access to public buildings such as hotels, offices and academic institutions is gained through an easily identified reception area, behind which lies a foyer and other access zones, as well as the further-reaching areas of use and access. The architecture of these areas must be clearly identifiable from a distance, and the lighting good enough to ensure visibility even under conditions of poor or non-existent daylight. > Fig. 31 Furthermore, an entrance serves as a transition zone between the inside and the outside. In other words, lighting design has to help the eye in latently adapting to the changing light situation. Daylight-dependent controls now prove their full value, providing powerful illumination during the day and adjusting the lighting at night to that of the darkness outside.

The illumination of entrance areas and foyers

If the building or the reception zone is accessed via stairs, the lighting must be illuminated accordingly so that the steps stand out from one another. In addition, the individual steps can be individually illuminated by recessed luminaires or strip lighting in order to emphasize the route.

In the foyer, the aim is to create a form of illumination that assists orientation. Additional accentuation can be achieved by illuminating individual areas such as the walls, ceilings, columns and the stairs. Above all, it is in multi-story foyers that pendant luminaires and ceiling luminaires

Tab. 9: Exemplary, necessary illumination intensities for public areas

Area	Luminance [lx]
Entrance/foyer (depending on the traffic)	100–200
Stairs	150
Waiting areas	500
Cash points/counters/bars	300–500
Shop windows	> 2,000
Supermarkets/DIY stores	> 1,000
Dining rooms/restaurants	200
Buffets/self-service counters	300

come into their own as a design element, since there is a multitude of brands to choose from. LED lamps are ideal for the routing and orientation because they generate warm-white and pure white colours – depending on the landscaping. > Fig. 31

If there are reception zones, reception desks and waiting areas, they should be viewed independently, since a greater luminous intensity is required in these areas than in the surrounding area.

The lighting of museums and exhibition rooms

The illumination of exhibition rooms presents light planners with one of their most complex tasks. Thanks to the architecture, the basic concepts have been defined here, since the basic concept has already been outlined: i.e. whether a pure art-light plan can be defined by the draft plan, whether a pure art-light plan is to be realized, or whether daylight is to be made available in the exhibition areas. The ground plans vary from hall-like spaces (with installations and mobile room dividers, in some cases) to smaller single rooms with clearly defined routes. In specific cases, the room measurements and heights, as well as the types of exhibit, call for special planning. Since museums and other exhibition areas often do not merely display a permanent collection, but have to rely on changing exhibitions, a considerable degree of flexibility is required with regard to the illumination (e.g. via live lines, mobile spotlights, and flexible grids). > Fig. 32

For the overall lighting, diffuse illumination is recommended: in other words, measures that take advantage of the daylight and artificial lighting. In this way, uniform room lighting can be achieved with a minimum amount of shadow. Ceiling luminaires and luminous ceilings with a diffuse covering (for example, frosted glass) are particularly suitable for this purpose. Owing to their longer operating life, fluorescent lamps are

Fig. 31: Examples of illumination in the entrance area and the foyer

Fig. 32: Examples of the illumination of museums and exhibitions

recommended, because they provide sufficient amounts of illumination and excellent visual impact. If visitors wish to move freely through the exhibition area without having to choose a specific direction, a more general form of illumination will suffice to start with. If there is a concept for guiding visitors around the exhibition, an additional constellation of path luminaires can be chosen in the form of floor and wall lamps, or in the design of strip lights.

In the next planning stage, the prime focus will be on the illumination of the exhibits themselves. Planning of this kind also depends greatly on the nature and material quality of the choice of exhibits. Paintings and pictures have to be handled quite differently from sculptures and showcases. Audio and video installations are increasingly being used as supportive media, or as art in themselves. All these exhibits share a common feature: they can be emphasized with highly focused lamps such as spotlights and downlights. It is worth noting that the visitor may well be focusing on a specific exhibit, without there being any reflections, shadows or glare. Radiation effects, which emanate from daylight, as well as artificial

Fig. 33: The illumination of exhibition objects

sources of light, can damage exhibition items and paintings in the long term, since they can trigger chemical processes. The latter must be minimized by using a suitable choice of illuminants and additional filters with the aim of diminishing infrared and ultraviolet radiation. If an exhibit is displayed in the wall area, the beam angle of the light concerned must be set at a slight angle of 25° to 30° to the lower edge of the exhibit.

The illumination
of restaurants

The illumination of restaurants varies considerably depending on the type of gastronomy. For example, a cafeteria offering self-service requires different lighting levels and light colours than a posh restaurant with a dining room. In this case, the planning tasks include general lighting, accent lighting, and the illumination of bars and tables, while in the case of restaurants, exterior lighting also plays a role: not only because gastronomy must be acknowledged as such, but also because the type and quality of the illumination influences customers' expectations even before they enter the restaurant.

The overall lighting generally assumes the form of ceiling lighting (as individual illumination, or in the shape of power rails with a number of directed spotlights). Additional ambient light and spatial designs can be introduced in the form of wall luminaires. In order to realize a variety of usage scenarios, plans should include variable illumination involving a dimmer and, in some cases, lighting that can be switched on and off as required. In self-service areas, far higher illumination levels (200 lx) will be provided than in a restaurant with service staff. Here, too, there is a lack of uniformity regarding illumination levels: some areas will be emphasized. In the lounges, the lighting is often supported – or even largely replaced – by accent lighting. The illumination of the room zones, columns, walls and individual objects, such as pictures and other features, is to be planned and integrated into the overall concept. > Fig.34 In the process, the lighting levels, light colours and, consequently, the choice of lamps

44

Fig. 34: The illumination of dining rooms, bars and buffets

Fig. 35: The illumination of restaurant tables

and lighting, may vary considerably. With regard to the illumination of a wall painting, completely different measures will have to be taken from those designed for accentuating glasses or porcelain.

Particularly bright-but-dazzle-free lighting should be chosen for the bar and buffet areas. > Fig. 34 These spheres generally serve as the main areas of contact for the guests and the working areas of the personnel. Lamps with a light colour rendering index are essential so that the guests can see and evaluate the food. Thermal radiation must be restricted, however. Low-pressure discharge lamps are particularly apt in this context and can be deployed, with reflectors, in a compact form, yet very large in number, in the areas described.

Fig. 36: Examples of shop-window illumination

Fig. 37: The illumination of sales areas

Restaurant tables are to be illuminated to a far greater degree than in the surrounding areas. Generally speaking, illumination of this type is created with pendant lights installed at heights of 50 cm to 70 cm above the table top. Lamps with a high colour rendering index are used, so that the food, as well as the other people at the table, can be clearly identified. On the whole, halogen lamps are used, which generate a warm-white light colour.

The illumination of the sales rooms and presentation lighting

In the case of the illumination plans for the sales rooms, the presentation area of the window is generally the main focal point. It is not only the initial area of contact, but also the first source of information for customers. In this case, illumination strengths of more than 1,000 lx are required, as well as, lights with good colour-reproduction properties, which means using high-pressure and low-pressure discharge lamps. In general, ceiling lamps are employed which feature modifiable systems adapted to suit the changing displays. Apart from widely scattered light designed for general illumination, individual products can be greatly accentuated via spotlights and downlights. By choosing suitable glazing with a minimal reflection share, an unhindered view of the display can be assured day and night. > Fig. 36

The type of sales area — in conjunction with the products to be sold — determines the lighting plan. People generally associate a variety of intensive illumination and light colours with familiar scenarios. Hence, for instance, sales areas equipped with a high level of illumination favour associations with discount supermarkets and DIY stores. Radiators and individual lights are merely used to draw attention to their very high-grade product ranges. The frequently monotonous architecture and the apparent lack of decorative effort involved (hence, inconspicuous from a builder's point of view) and an economical approach to resources have been adopted, allowing companies to offer their customers the best sales prices. > Fig. 37 With low illumination densities, warm light colours accentuate of certain sub-domains, so customers unconsciously feel that the goods on display are of high quality and deserve special attention. In the same vein, counters displaying food in a wide range of colours suggest fresh quality by displaying, for example, white light with salads and vegetables, and red tones with meat products. As the greater part of the sales areas involves products that change every week or season, and are, therefore, repeatedly positioned anew, flexible illumination systems — especially where accent lighting is concerned — are advisable. ■

The cash points, information counters and individual counters for customer enquiries (in a furniture store, for example) ought to be treated separately, since, on the one hand, the routes for the customers are clearly laid out whereas, on the other hand, guidelines for workplace illumination have to be followed, as the sales personnel largely remain in these fields.

■ **Tip:** Depending on the product, the type of illuminant and the light colour, the lamps, the luminous colour and the nature of the lamps, dazzling effects and reflections can be created or avoided. Items of clothing and furniture ought to be illuminable without such effects, whereas in the case of exhibited wares, such as jewellery and technical products, sparkle and reflection lend these products a more sophisticated and modern look.

WORKSTATIONS

The most common task in lighting design lies in the planning of work-places. Whereas the overriding concern in lighting design for living spaces tends to involve the subjective feelings of the users and the design aspects, far-reaching and comprehensive demands and guidelines have to be demanded of workplaces, which have to be considered in the planning and are frequently stated as the planning goal. As a rule – and inasmuch as the stipulations and spatial orientation permit – a combination of daylight and artificial light will be used to achieve a constant level of brightness in the face of changing weather conditions.

In this field, visual tasks determine the nature and intensity of the required lighting. In the case of a one-person-office workstation, very different planning elements are required in order to make available the necessary illumination factors, which differ from those encountered in industrial factories and laboratories.

The office workstation Office workstations are subject to norms and guidelines concerning illumination intensities. Hence, the illuminance level for artificial light is cited as 500 lx; in the particular case of a <u>daylight-oriented workstation</u>, it lies at 300 lx. In addition to the overall room illumination, a workspace/workplace always has to be viewed separately and, if sufficient illumination cannot be obtained via the central room lighting, it will have to be equipped with additional lamps. The size and position of the windows provide the ideal zone for setting up a workstation in the office, because the high light densities typically required for visual tasks are reached next to the windows, whereas the deeper-lying zones are more suitable for storage space, cupboards and other uses involving less demanding visual tasks. Hence, the spread of light in an interior room can be determined via simple rules. Areas are considered bright when they lie within a 30° angle to the upper edge of the window or beneath an upper skylight. > Fig. 38 In order to make a room flexible and usable, a window's width has to occupy at least 55 % of the room's width and the window's surface area in the facade must account for at least 30 %. Other influences, such as trees, the construction of neighbouring buildings, and so on, must be taken into account here, since they can mean that light propagation is limited (in direction or intensity) in comparison with other equally oriented rooms.

The desired and largely necessary use of daylight for workplaces generally involves antiglare measures being taken on all window surfaces, and often involves carrying out additional solar protection measures too. Furthermore, blending, which arises from the direct or reflecting effects of lamps, must be avoided. The office workstation itself – which takes its orientation from the monitors and lamps – should be set up so that the

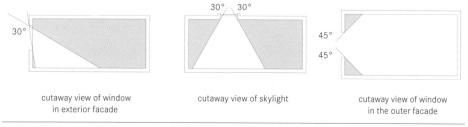

| cutaway view of window in exterior facade | cutaway view of skylight | cutaway view of window in the outer facade |

Fig. 38: The natural illumination of a workstation

Fig. 39: The illumination of an office workstation

direction of the user's gaze runs parallel to the windows. The working environment (i.e., the desk, the walls and the ceilings) should be equipped with light-coloured matte surfaces to ensure a high degree of reflection — but an absence of reflected glare. The main working area should also be equipped with its own individually adjustable lighting, as well as desk lamps and/or individually controllable standing lamps, because — alongside the generally regulated minimum standards — the user-requirements different greatly. In the case of office spaces alongside a workspace proper, which is devoted to more complex visual tasks such as writing, reading, and so on, additional lamps will be provided in order to generate the necessary amount of light.

Ideally, additional artificial lighting in the workplace should be regulated by a light control system tied to the presence of people in the room and light. By integrating sun protection measures into the control system, it would be possible to run an economical as well as an optimally tuned light concept designed for maximum comfort.

Fig. 40: The illumination of conference rooms

A special, planned case, which is becoming increasingly common, is that of the daylight-oriented workplace. This means that for at least 70 % of the working hours, daylight – without the addition of artificial light – provides sufficient illumination. This value is directly dependent on daylight factor D, since a higher daylight quotient already implies a lower degree of dependence on supplementary artificial illumination. It can be roughly estimated that with a daylight factor of more than 3 % per day, a high-quality daylight-oriented workplace can be created.

Conference room/
meetings

In conference rooms, the lighting design must ensure that all of the participants can be easily identified from each and every position. The conference table is usually placed in a central position vis-à-vis the ceiling or the pendant lamps. The luminaires must direct their light laterally, without creating any glare. > Fig. 40 Inside the room, care must be taken to avoid stark contrasts in brightness caused by the general lighting and the surface qualities, since contrasts of this nature can create fatigue among participants even when they are in a peripheral area.

Industrial factory halls

In industrial halls running production processes, lighting design depends on the nature of the visual tasks and the hall's geometry. In the case of a high room, powerful lamps, such as metal high-pressure steam lamps, high-pressure sodium lamps and fluorescent lamps, will be needed to generate a sufficient degree of illumination at the place of work. If the hall's ceiling is lower (less than 6.00 m), fluorescent lamps arranged in screens — or strip lighting/lights — will be ideal. If fluorescent lights are used, care must be taken to ensure they are aligned parallel to the working surface in order to avoid glare. Illumination intensities of 1,500 lx have to be reached in order to create a working ambience conducive to productivity and an environment that prevents accidents. Most industrial

Fig. 41: The illumination of industrial factory halls

workplaces have illumination intensities of 600 lx and neutral white colours. If emissions occur during indoor operation (e.g., from dust or similar pollution), steps must be taken to ensure that sufficient protection is taken when using lamps.

As it is normally impossible to rely on natural illumination via the facade openings in a factory hall, the daylight entering the skylights is generally used. > Fig. 41 Given the available daylight, a control is needed to lessen the economic burden caused by permanently using artificial light, which can represent a considerable cost-factor in a large business. Electronic ballast units can increase cost-effectiveness, especially in factories operating on a shift-work basis and high switch-on times.

When people are working in <u>warehouses</u>, lower illumination levels are needed than is the case in production sites and factories using industrial processes. The nature of the hall, as well as its use, determines the required lighting level. > Tab.10 Reflector luminaires are frequently used as strip lighting in combination with fluorescent lamps, which, along with

Tab. 10: The required illumination intensities of diverse packing rooms

Type of storage	Luminance level [lx]
Storage spaces for large stocks of the same item	50
Storage spaces for varied goods	100
Storage spaces with reading functions	200
Dispatch and packing room	300

Fig. 42: Examples of warehouse lighting

directed reflectors, adequately illuminate corridors, shelves and stored merchandise, and also offer protection against glare if looked at directly. Furthermore, a motion controller is advisable in storage areas that are not permanently used. Please note that in the desk area and other work-places involving visual tasks of greater complexity, supplementary illumi-nation must be provided that is similar to the office working space.

EMERGENCY AND SAFETY LIGHTING

To facilitate orientation in the case of a disruption to the main power supply, an emergency (or security) lighting source is necessary in spe-cific cases. This applies to public areas in which the identification and visibility of the emergency and escape routes must be secured perma-nently so that people can escape in situations of danger. As a rule, the emergency escape routes are identified by self-illuminating rescue signs. In battery mode, the escape routes are controlled by a special power cir-cuit designed to ensure that signage continues to function. Escape route signs/pictograms that are not supplied by electricity, but dispose of phos-phorescent surfaces, can be allowed if this is explained in the fire-pro-tection concept. > Fig. 43 In the case of escape-route lighting, a minimum illumination intensity of 1 lux must be ensured for a distance of 2.0 m. To ensure that escape is possible, a specified level must be reached – i.e., illuminance of 40 lux – along the course of the middle line of the escape route.

In the case of workstations with special requirements, where there is a danger of the illumination failing, the security illumination must be designed on such a scale that leaving the place of work and even ending a necessary job is possible.

Fig. 43: Examples of emergency and security illumination

THE ILLUMINATION OF PRIVATE SPACES

The illumination of private rooms is less structured than it is in the preceding scenarios. In this case, it is more the wishes and feelings of the inhabitants and users that determines the planning definitions. Furthermore, the way a room is used may differ from case to case. For example, the functions performed by a living room can vary greatly from one user to another.

The external impact of a building at dusk and night is shaped by the illumination of the facade, the garden and the entrance area. In addition to any design aspects, the illumination of the access routes and the entrance area serves as orientation and security. Diverse entrance situations can make various types of illuminants worthwhile. Hence, if there is a porch, lamps can be integrated above the house door, otherwise various wall lamps can be fitted in the facade. Access to building entrances and garages, as well as steps, pedestals and external stairs, should certainly be illuminated. Bollard luminaires and plinths, as well as lamps that have been integrated into the ground, are most qualified for this task. It is important to ensure that the pathway illumination avoids light-and-dark contrasts and clearly identifies obstacles. In this case, the distance between the lamps should be adjusted to match the selected height of the light source and the direction of the beam. In the case of light columns, a larger distance can be chosen than is the case with pendant luminaires. House numbers can also be designed as self-illuminating objects or beamed via a single lamp, if the customary illumination is otherwise not powerful enough, or if the number needs to be permanently emphasized.

> Fig. 44

Home illumination and garden illumination

Fig. 44 The illumination of the house and the facade

In contrast to a semi-public entrance area, a garden can display far greater contrasts in order to emphasize certain spots and objects. As a rule, a garden needs direct accentuation and focus rather than wide-scale general illumination. In this case, the desired atmosphere can be attained with light and dark areas. The general sense of security can be enhanced by motion-controlled lighting. In order to illuminate features such as trees and other solitary objects, such as sculptures, well-directed spotlights are ideally suited. The distance must be adapted to the size – or to the magnitude – of the object to be emphasized. The alignment of the illumination should be planned in a way that avoids glare.

As with the illumination of open public spaces, here, too, it is absolutely necessary to pay attention to the use of illuminants with an appropriate protection class.

When selecting an illuminant, the type of switch and the time of the switching are overriding factors. If a certain feature, such as a house door, is to be permanently illuminated, it is advisable to use economical LEDs or compact fluorescent lamps. To this end, twilight switches and time switches can be used, which automatically regulate the illumination. In the case of shorter switching cycles, as in the case of a motion detector or a push switch, halogen lamps and energy-saving lamps can be used. Please note that when using motion detectors on paths, illuminants should be used that release their full luminous flux immediately after the lighting has been switched on, and without a long interim phase, in order
■   to ensure their immediate accessibility.

The living room   Suitable lighting of a living room depends upon the room's geometry, the size of the windows, and the furnishings, as well as the specific uses of the room. Superordinate general lighting, combined with court-

Fig. 45: Living room illumination

yard lighting of the sofas and a lounge unit, as well as accentuation of other elements, calls for thorough planning. The visual axes must be defined to exclude glare and to clearly lay down the positioning of the luminaires. Reflections on objects such as televisions, pictures and so on, are to be avoided.

The overall illumination should be kept separate from the additional single lamps and be dimmable. The desired brightness should be emitted not via a single lamp but via several well-distributed lamps. Since these lamps can differ greatly from one another in the various areas, wall and ceiling lamps can be used just as well as spotlights on power rails and pendant luminaires. Particularly suitable here is lighting viewed as "comfortable", such as warm-white sources. The illumination of squares and outside areas can be supplemented by dimmable individual lamps, standard lamps and table lamps, allowing the user to adjust the brightness to his or her liking. Very often, uplights are used to enhance the level of the general illumination in certain parts of the room. Additional sources of accent lighting, aimed at highlighting features such as artworks, plants, furniture, as well as wall and ceiling surfaces, can be provided via downlights and spotlights. > Fig. 45

■ **Tip:** Light planning of the external domain of private buildings is to be undertaken and coordinated at an early stage of the planning, because many of the components required for electrical installations (cable routes, connections for a sub-distribution unit, etc.) have to be laid under plaster during an early stage of the construction work. Planning external installations and other jobs late in the day generally results in inconvenience and causes delays in subsequent installations.

Fig. 46: The illumination of the dining table

Dining room /
dining table

As in restaurants and cafés, the main focus of a dining room illumination is the dining table. Here, general illumination plays more of a subordinate role: it is, however, important to allow for a certain degree of orientation when the dining table is not being used, or rather: when the dining table illumination is not being used. In larger dining rooms, however, additional and general degrees of illumination must be provided – independently of the table lighting. The number and design of the table illuminations is to be adapted to the size, form and material of the table. Very often, pendant luminaires are used. In this case, they should be hung slightly above eye-level. As with diverse choices of dining room furniture, luminaires are supplied in almost all forms and materials. > Fig. 46

The kitchen

In the kitchen, there is a need to see clearly into cupboards and shelves. Thus, there is a need for more powerful illumination than is the case in other rooms. This applies to the general lighting as well as the illumination of the working surfaces. General lighting ought to be managed via a number of light sources, in order to ensure there is sufficient brightness in all parts of the kitchen. On the whole, the ceiling illumination will consist of an extension in the form of a surface-mounted luminaire or a fitted spotlight with warm-white lamps. In the working areas, the illumination will have to be even more powerful, to ensure a level of brightness appropriate for kitchen work. The same applies to the colour rendering index $R_a > 90$, so that the foodstuffs, including their state and quality, can be easily seen. The additional illuminated working surfaces can be organized via directed spotlights, downlights and individual spots, which can, for example, be arranged beneath the top kitchen cupboards. Their position must be chosen so that users don't create shadows when they are working on these surfaces. Nobody who is working in a kitchen should be distracted by the lighting. The area around the stove and oven also needs additional illumination, which can, in many cases, be integrated into an extractor hood. Owing to the occasionally intense presence of fat,

Fig. 47: Kitchen Illumination

liquids and so on, covers that are illuminated and easy-to-clean-and-dis-mantle are ideal. Kitchen cupboards can always be cleaned separately, so the illumination in these areas can be switched on and off via door contact. The illumination of bars and dining tables in the kitchen domain can be effected in much the same way as the dining table illumination.
> Fig. 47   ○

In addition to illuminating the mirror surfaces and cosmetic areas, The bathroom standard lighting with a high degree of illumination intensity and a good colour rendering index (R_a > 90) is provided in the bathrooms. Depending on the materials used for the surfaces (gloss or matte tiles, the tile colours, the number and size of the mirror surfaces), a great deal of reflection may be caused by the illumination. For this reason, the number of lamps, as well as their illumination intensity, will vary even in bathrooms with the same dimensions. In order to avoid glare, measures must be taken to spread the light by choosing appropriate light covering.

○ **Note:** In order to integrate illuminations into the furnishings and fixtures – such as kitchen cupboards, shelves and other items of furniture – it is essential that the selected illuminations be provided with a MM mark. To this end, these illuminations are defined as devices with a limited surface temperature, thus providing the necessary fire protection.

Fig. 48: Bathroom illumination and mirror luminaires

Fig. 49: The illumination of the stair flights and steps

For general lighting, primarily ceiling illumination should be used. It is, therefore, important to note where people stand or sit (in front of the washbasin or the bathtub, for example) in order to avoid undesirable shadows or glare. Additional illuminations with light-scattering properties should be planned above the mirrors, or on both sides of them. As these illuminations have to attain far greater illumination strengths than standard lighting, more economical illuminants — such as LEDs and energy-saving lamps — are recommended. > Fig. 48

As bathrooms are often damp or wet areas, special lamps providing adequate protection should be used. With respect to the electrical installations, it is essential that only approved materials be used. Furthermore, general illumination must render wet areas clearly in order to avoid accidents.

When planning the illumination of stairs, it is imperative to regard them as traffic routes and to be aware that failure to use a sufficient luminance level (100 lux) is impermissible. First and foremost, general and constant illumination is absolutely essential, and the additional development and accentuation of individual steps permissible. The overall illumination of a staircase should begin from above: via the walls and the ceiling luminaires. In order to achieve an equal distribution of light, a number of broadly radiating or light-diffusing lamps can be used. > Fig. 49

The position of the stairs also plays a key role in light planning, especially when it comes to switching the lighting on and off, because a staircase that is frequently used by many people is easier to regulate with individual switches, or with motion detectors using time-controlled switching. In this case, the safety of people using the stairs must be guaranteed. Lamps can be switched on or off in combination with the illumination of an adjacent room.

In Conclusion

Successful lighting design calls for a rigorous debate on the planning tasks throughout every phase of the work. In addition to taking into consideration the wishes expressed by the client, the demands arising from the various guidelines and standards, as well as the lighting's location and use, it is essential, above all, to constantly re-examine and adapt the specific conditions of the project within the overall framework of light. Now that the design concept is completed and the specialized companies have been commissioned, care must be taken that during the course of construction the planned interaction between daylight and artificial light, as well as the interweaving of the individual planning elements, is realized as planned and in line with the standards for the varied elements' subsequent operation. The preparation of simulations during the design process serves to clarify the planned measures for the user, and ensures that the required standards of luminance are adhered to and that the structure is actually built as planned. However, it is always essential to allow for a certain degree of flexibility during the planning phase.

Appendix

LITERATURE

Andreas Achilles, Diane Navratil: *Basics Glass Construction,* Birkhäuser Verlag, Basel 2008

Bert Bielefeld (ed.): Planning Architecture: *Dimensions and Typologies,* Birkhäuser Verlag, Basel 2016

Mohamed Boubekri: *Daylighting Design: Planning Strategies and Best Practice Solutions,* Birkhäuser Verlag, Basel 2014

Ulrike Brandi Licht: *Detail Practice: Lighting Design: Principles, Implementation, Case Studies,* Edition DETAIL, München 2006

Ulrike Brandi: *Light for Cities: Lighting Design for Urban Spaces. A Handbook,* Birkhäuser Verlag, Basel 2006

Ulrike Brandi, Christoph Geissmar-Brandi: *Lightbook: The Practice of Lighting Design,* Birkhäuser Verlag, Basel 2001

Hans-Georg Buschendorf (ed.): *Lexikon Licht- und Beleuchtungstechnik,* Verlag Technik, Berlin 1989

Andrea Deplazes (ed.): *Constructing Architecture,* 3rd edition, Birkhäuser Verlag, Basel 2013

Jill Entwistle: *Detail in Contemporary Lighting Design,* Laurence King Publishing, London 2012

Doris Haas-Arndt, Fred Ranft: *Tageslichttechnik in Gebäuden*, Hüthig Jehle Rehm, Heidelberg 2007

Gerhard Hausladen, Petra Liedl, Michael de Saldanha: *Building to Suit the Climate.* A Handbook, Birkhäuser Verlag, Basel 2012

Manfred Hegger e.a.: Aktivhaus. *The Reference Work,* Birkhäuser Verlag, Basel 2016

Roland Krippner, Florian Musso: *Basics Facade Apertures,* Birkhäuser Verlag, Basel 2007

Vincent Laganier, Jasmine van der Pol (eds.): *Light and Emotions. Exploring Lighting Cultures,* Birkhäuser Verlag, Basel 2011

Wolfram Pistohl, Christian Rechenauer, Birgit Scheuerer: *Handbuch der Gebäudetechnik*, Band 2: *Heizung | Lüftung | Beleuchtung | Energiesparen*, 8. Auflage, Werner Verlag, Cologne 2013

Alexander Reichel, Kerstin Schultz (eds.): *Scale: Open | Close. Windows, Doors, Gates, Loggias, Filters,* Birkhäuser Verlag, Basel 2009

Hans Rudolf Ris: *Beleuchtungstechnik für Praktiker,* VDE, Berlin 2015

Wolfgang M. Willems (ed.): *Lehrbuch der Bauphysik: Schall – Wärme – Feuchte – Licht – Brand – Klima,* 7. Auflage, Springer Vieweg, Wiesbaden 2013

Sage Russell: *The Architecture Of Light: A textbook of procedures and practices for the Architect, Interior Designer and Lighting Designer*, 2nd edition, Conceptnine 2012

Peter Tregenza, David Loe: *The Design of Lighting,* 2 edition, Routledge, London 2013

Peter Wotschke: *Basics Electro-Planning,* Birkhäuser Verlag, Basel 2017

STANDARDS

European Standards
BS EN 1838 "Emergency lighting"
BS EN 12464-1:2011-08 Title: "Light and lighting – Lighting of work places" – Part 1: Indoor work places; German Version EN 12464-1:2011
BS EN 12464-2:2014-05 Title: "Light and lighting – Lighting of work places" – Part 2: Outdoor work places; German version EN 12464-2:2014
BS EN 12665 "Light and lighting – Basic terms and criteria for specifying lighting requirements"
BS EN 13032 "Light and lighting – Measurement and presentation of photometric data of lamps and luminaires"
BS EN 13201 "Road lighting"
BS EN 60529:2014-09 "Degrees of protection provided by enclosures" (IP Code) (IEC 60529:1989 + A1:1999 + A2:2013); German version EN 60529:1991 + A1:2000 + A2:2013
BS EN 60598-1:2015-10; VDE 0711-1:2015-10; "Luminaires" – Part 1: General requirements and tests (IEC 60598-1:2014, modified); German version EN 60598-1:2015

German Standards
DIN 5034 "Daylight in interiors"
DIN 5035 "Artificial lighting"

Guidelines
VDI 6011 "Lighting technology – Optimisation of daylight use and artificial lighting – Fundamentals and basic requirements"
ASR A3.4 Lighting

PICTURE CREDITS

Fig. 6, left: Feans, flickr.com

Fig. 7, left: Roman Pfeiffer, flickr.com

Fig. 17: Sebastian Terfloth, User: Sese_Ingolstadt – Eigenes Werk, licensed by CC-SA-3.0 via Wikimedia Commons – https://commons.wikimedia.org/wiki/File:Lounge_ICE_3.jpg

Fig. 19, right, User Ozguy89, licensed by GNU Free Documentation License, transferred from en.wikipedia to Commons by User: Wdwd using CommonsHelper, – https://commons.wikimedia.org/wiki/File:150_Watt_Metal_Halide.jpg

Fig. 25, centre: Walter Schärer, flickr.com, processed

Fig. 33, left: C MB 166, flickr.com

Fig. 43, right: David Hollnack

The author thanks Bogdan Napieralski for helping with the preparation of the photographs for Figs. 4, centre; 22, right; 27; 28; 30 left+right

THE AUTHOR

Dipl.-Ing. Architect Roman Skowranek is working as an architect in Dortmund.

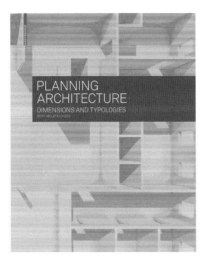

Bert Bielefeld (Ed.)

Planning Architecture
Dimensions and Typologies

SEITEN	568
FORMAT	24,0 × 30,0 cm
PRINT GEB.	EUR [D] 119.95 / USD 149.95/ GBP 89.99 978-3-0356-0323-1 EN
PRINT BR.	EUR [D] 69.95 / USD 84.95/ GBP 52.99 978-3-0356-0324-8 EN

In formulating a design concept into a viable plan, architects oscillate constantly between two planes of observation: the actual design task in the context of planning typologies such as residential buildings, office buildings, museum, or airport, and the individual room, meaning the kitchen, office, classroom, sanitary rooms, storage rooms, and so on. *Planning Architecture* offers architects and students a well thought-out planning tool, in which two main sections reciprocally complement one another:

the "spaces" and the "typologies" between which the planner can flexibly oscillate depending on his or her plane of observation. All relevant planning information is presented in a detailed clear fashion, and in context.

These two sections are flanked by an introductory chapter explaining the basis and framework for typological design, as well as a "reference section" at the end of the book that clearly lists general dimensions and units, regulations and standards.

Series editor: Bert Bielefeld

Concept: Bert Bielefeld, Annette Gref

Translation from German into English:
Robin Benson

English copy editing: John Sweet

Project management: Silke Martini, Lisa Schulze

Layout, cover design and typography:
Andreas Hidber

Typesetting: Sven Schrape

Production: Heike Strempel

Library of Congress Cataloging-in-Publication
data
A CIP catalogue record for this book has been
applied for at the Library of Congress.

Bibliographic information published by the
German National Library
The German National Library lists this publication in the Deutsche Nationalbibliografie;
detailed bibliographic data are available on
the Internet at http://dnb.dnb.de.

This publication is also available as an e-book
(ISBN PDF 978-3-0356-1289-9; ISBN EPUB
978-3-0356-1302-5) and in a German language
edition (ISBN 978-3-0356-0929-5).

© 2017 Birkhäuser Verlag GmbH, Basel
P.O. Box 44, 4009 Basel, Switzerland
Part of Walter de Gruyter GmbH, Berlin/Boston

Printed on acid-free paper produced from
chlorine-free pulp. TCF ∞

Printed in Germany

ISBN 978-3-0356-0930-1

9 8 7 6 5 4 3 2 1

www.birkhauser.com